Animal Physical Therapist

Trudi Strain Trueit

Cavendish
Square

New York

Published in 2014 by Cavendish Square Publishing, LLC
303 Park Avenue South, Suite 1247, New York, NY 10010

Copyright © 2014 by Cavendish Square Publishing, LLC

First Edition

Library of Congress Cataloging-in-Publication Data

Trueit, Trudi Strain.
Animal physical therapist / by Trudi Strain Trueit.
p. cm. — (Careers with animals)
Includes index.
ISBN 978-1-62712-458-4 (hardcover) ISBN 978-1-62712-459-1 (paperback) ISBN 978-1-62712-460-7 (ebook)
1. Veterinary physical therapy — Juvenile literature. 2. Veterinary medicine — Vocational guidance —Juvenile literature. I. Trueit, Trudi Strain. II. Title.
SF925 T74 2014
636.7—dc23

Editorial Director: Dean Miller
Senior Editor: Peter Mavrikis
Copy Editor: Cynthia Roby
Art Director: Jeffrey Talbot
Designer: Amy Greenan
Photo Researcher: Julie Alissi, J8 Media
Production Manager: Jennifer Ryder-Talbot
Production Editor: Andrew Coddington

CONTENTS

ONE

Creature Comforts

Freckles was in bad shape. The cute, blond cocker spaniel had undergone spinal surgery for a herniated disk (one of the soft cushions that sits between the vertebrae of the spine had slipped out of place, causing pain and paralysis). It had been six weeks since the operation and Freckles should have been up and around, but she wasn't. Her hind legs were still paralyzed. Freckles' veterinarian referred her owners to Julie Stuart, a licensed physical therapist, who worked with animals.

When Julie examined the eight-year-old dog, she found little sensation and no movement in Freckles' back legs. Yet, she wasn't discouraged. "I felt confident we could get her walking again," says Julie. "We needed to help her regain strength in her spinal muscles as well as in her legs. We also needed to give her lots of sensory input on her back legs with the hope that with practice, the signals would get through the area of damage in her spinal cord and she would begin feeling her legs again." In this case, sensory input meant stimulating the nerves through touch, such as massage, brushing, tickling, or scratching.

Julie created a physical therapy treatment program for Freckles. Three days each week she worked with the dog, doing sensory training, stretching, and passive range of motion (moving the dog's legs for her). Strength training

(Opposite) Classed as a toy dog breed because of its small size, this Pomeranian waits for its therapy session with its owner.

An animal physical therapist's relationship and interaction with patients can play an important role in long-term wellness.

included pinching the toes for reflex withdrawal and helping Freckles to stand and shift her weight. Each session lasted about an hour. Julie also gave Freckles' owners "homework," exercises to do with their dog between her visits. Within a month or so, the cocker spaniel had gained strength. She was able to bear more weight on her legs. After two months, Julie saw the first signs of voluntary motion. "It was so exciting!" she recalls.

Slowly, Julie began helping the dog to take her first steps. Each week brought a little more improvement. As Freckles progressed, Julie added more strength exercises, balance exercises, gait (walk) retraining, and **hydrotherapy** in the form of swimming. In six months, Freckles was walking by herself and

Do You Have What It Takes?

Animal physical therapy might be the right career for you, if you...

- have a strong desire to help animals and their owners
- are patient and don't easily lose your temper
- are compassionate to the suffering of others
- are a determined and creative problem-solver
- enjoy science, math, and English and can earn top grades in these areas
- are willing to spend seven to eight years in college, and continue your education throughout your career

Animal physical therapists oftentimes prescribe exercise as part of a treatment plan for recovering animals.

even climbing stairs again. The treatment program was a success! Julie, however, is quick to give her patient much of the credit. "It was an amazing experience to watch her work so hard and to be such a good sport about her workouts with me. To this day, we still say, 'Freckles was such a hard worker!'"

Animal physical rehabilitation practitioners, or animal physical therapists as they are called more informally, help restore normal function to an animal's joints and muscles. They work with a patient to improve strength, balance, flexibility, and gait. They also help manage pain and prevent future injuries. Practitioners may use one or more techniques to accomplish these goals, including **therapeutic exercise,** stretching, strength training, massage, and hydrotherapy. Some learn to use **acupuncture** and **chiropractic** as well. Physical therapy can help animals heal from surgery, bounce back from an injury, combat obesity, or handle the effects of aging. It can dramatically improve the quality of life for dogs, cats, horses, and many other kinds of animals.

Birth of a Profession

Animal physical rehabilitation as a profession is less than fifty years old. But its roots go deep. It stems from the practice of physical therapy for humans, which can be traced back thousands of years. The ancient Chinese perfected the use of acupuncture, massage, herbs, and heat in treating illness and injury in humans. Ancient Greek gymnasts were among the first to use therapeutic exercise to help injured athletes. A Greek doctor named Hippocrates (460 BC – 370 BC), who is considered the father of modern medicine, recognized the healing properties of water and massage.

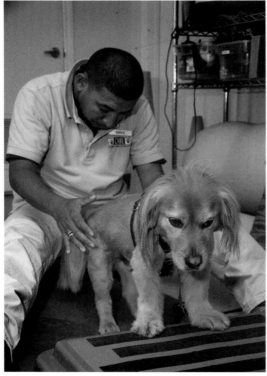

As part of the treatment plan for a back injury, this dog has his hindquarter massaged by a Santa Monica, California, veterinary technician.

In the early twentieth century, a national **polio** outbreak, along with thousands of injured and disabled soldiers returning home from World War I, highlighted the need for trained physical therapists in the United States. Veterinarians saw how effective the approach was for people and began adapting it for their four-footed patients. Animal athletes were the first to benefit. By the mid-1960s, injured racehorses and greyhounds were mending with help from massage, exercise, and **thermotherapy**, or the use of heat or cold. In the early 1990s, veterinarians and physical therapists began treating companion

Paving the Way

The University of Tennessee was the first college in the United States to offer a certificate program in animal physical therapy for medical professionals. Cofounded in 2001 by Dr. Daryl Millis and Dr. David Levine, the university's Canine Rehabilitation program welcomes veterinarians, veterinary technicians, physical therapists, and physical therapist assistants from across the nation and around the world. The two-week summer class provides hands-on training in massage, therapeutic exercise, joint mobilization, pain management, and more. "It's been received really well because it combines a couple of loves—the desire to help and the love of animals," says Dr. Levine. Students must also do a **practicum** and pass a final exam to receive certification. So far, about 2,000 students have taken classes and more than 500 have graduated from the program.

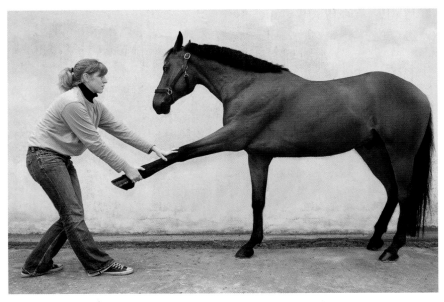

Equine osteopathy has proved useful in treatments of problems including maintaining mobility, reduced performance, and stiffness in different areas of the body. Once blockages are found and corrected, the body is restored to health.

animals, too. At the University of Tennessee, Dr. Darryl Millis, who taught veterinary orthopedic surgery, and physical therapy professor, Dr. David Levine, teamed up to teach some of the first courses in **canine** rehabilitation in the country. "Physical therapy was common for dogs and horses in racing," explains Dr. Levine. "So we thought, why not apply these same principles to dogs and small animals? Why not improve their quality of life? We have the ability to make a difference and we can do more than what we're doing."

Dr. Levine says most animal physical therapists don't intentionally choose it as a career. Instead, they discover this emerging field while studying to be a veterinarian or physical therapist (the profession is still so new, no college or university in the United States yet offers an advanced degree program that leads to a license). This is just what happened to Julie Stuart. In 1998, she was studying to become a physical therapist for humans when her golden retriever puppy, Tucker, was diagnosed with hip dysplasia (an abnormal formation of the hip socket). Veterinarians told her that Tucker would need hip replacement once he was grown. From her studies, Julie knew this kind of surgery would require significant physical therapy, so she set out to learn as much as she could to help her dog. After taking a course in canine physical therapy at the University of Tennessee, Julie found her life's calling: a career that blended her desire to work in physical therapy with her love of animals. She also discovered that if she set to work strengthening the muscles around Tucker's hips and put him on a regular exercise program, he might be able to avoid surgery.

Upon completion of her physical therapy degree, Julie took more canine rehabilitation classes and observed numerous veterinary surgeries. She began providing physical therapy to animal patients at The Cummings School of Veterinary Medicine at Tufts University near Boston, Massachusetts. She then opened her own private practice. Dogs are her primary focus, though Julie has treated horses, goats, llamas, zebras, and even a wallaby! Today, her passion for the career she stumbled into remains as strong as ever. "To make a difference in the lives of dogs and their owners is so rewarding," she says.

As for Tucker, the golden retriever led a full, active life and never did need a hip replacement.

TWO

Mapping an Education

Joining a profession just as it is blossoming can be exciting, but it can also present some challenges. The two biggest issues facing those wanting a career in animal physical rehabilitation are education and state licensing laws. We'll get to the state regulations in a moment, but first let's look at training.

As we've mentioned, at present, no college programs in animal physical rehabilitation exist in the United States for those seeking a degree in the field. Professionals say students who want to pursue the career should graduate from a four-year college or university, then continue on to either veterinary college or physical therapy school. Each track, however, has its pros and cons. Veterinary college provides an in-depth education of animals and their diseases, yet tends to offer limited instruction in physical therapy. On the other hand, a physical therapy curriculum covers the area well, but doesn't include study of or contact with animals. Whichever path students choose, they will need to fill in the gaps in their training with additional coursework, reading, observation, **internships**, and **externships**.

Which one should you choose? It depends on what you want to do as a professional. A physical therapist treats people and sometimes animals but is not allowed to **diagnose** illness and injury. Rather, he/she evaluates a patient

(Opposite) Students enrolled in an advanced animal science class at Snohomish High School in Snohomish, Washington, provide basic health exams for a variety of pets.

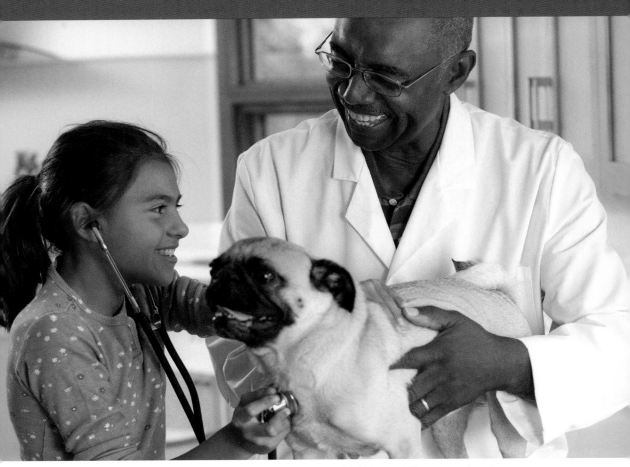

This future animal physical therapist examines a bulldog while a veterinarian assists her in learning.

referred by a doctor or veterinarian then creates and executes a physical therapy treatment plan. A veterinarian treats only animals, but he/she may tackle every phase of an animal's care, from initial diagnosis to surgery to physical therapy. If you want to treat people as well as animals in your practice, then being a physical therapist may be the right fit for you. If your goal is to treat illness and injury in animals, as well as provide physical therapy services for them, being a veterinarian is advised.

Before you make your decision, however, it's wise to research the licensing laws in your state. Regardless of whether they work with animals or people, all medical practitioners in the United States are required to have a license. A handful of states, such as Colorado, Nevada, Utah, and New Hampshire, recognize animal physical therapy as a profession. But many states do not. Some state laws are vague about defining what kind of patients practitioners may treat, while others clearly spell out that physical therapists are allowed to treat only people. "Some PTs [physical therapists] have been threatened with losing their licenses because they treat animals," explains Amie Hesbach, a licensed physical therapist and president of the American Physical Therapist Society's Animal Rehabilitation Special Interest Group. "It's a messy situation and it needs to get sorted out." To learn about the law where you live, check with the licensing board in your state. The Federation of State Boards of Physical Therapy has a list of all fifty boards and their websites online. Most states post their physical therapy practice acts on the Internet. If the wording for your state is unclear or vague, write to the state board for clarification of the law.

No matter which direction you choose, ultimately, you will want to learn as much as possible about both veterinary medicine and physical therapy. We'll explore each track in greater detail, but first let's look at the road to take to high school graduation.

What You Can Do Now

Middle and high school students interested in animal physical therapy should focus their studies on college preparatory math, science, health, and English. Math classes should include algebra, geometry, calculus, and statistics. In the sciences, take biology, chemistry, physics, and zoology. Look for health courses that focus on exercise science and **kinesiology**, or how the body moves. Enroll in English composition and literature, as well as a foreign language. Communication arts, psychology, business, web design, and computer courses are also recommended. Students should maintain a grade point average of 3.0 or above (the higher, the better). It's also a good idea to join clubs that involve math, science, leadership, business, and public speaking. Activities outside of school should include 4-H Youth Development, Future Farmers of America, or a pre-veterinary club.

Experts say it's good for middle and high school students to get experience working with animals other than their pets. Look for opportunities to volunteer at a veterinary clinic, rehabilitation hospital, shelter, sanctuary, farm, or zoo. Shadow, or observe, a physical therapist (one that treats animals is preferable). Keep a journal of all your volunteer activities and log service hours. Applications to veterinary colleges and physical therapy programs will ask about prior work experience. Students are also required to submit two to four letters of recommendation with their application, one or two of which will come from a past supervisor.

Students should decide between veterinary medicine and physical therapy while in high school, if possible. We'll explain why in a moment. Physical therapists complete a four-year college program to earn their bachelor's degree. After graduation, they enroll in three years of physical therapy school to receive a doctor of physical therapy (DPT). Veterinarians must take two to three years of college level **prerequisites**, or required classes. Veterinary schools in the United States do not require students to have a bachelor's degree. However, they strongly recommend it. A degree can give a student a competitive edge when applying to veterinary school. Also, it allows for other options should a student choose not to complete a veterinary program. Current statistics reveal 82 percent of students entering veterinary school have a bachelor's degree. The completion of prerequisite coursework or a degree is then followed by four years of study at veterinary college to earn a doctor of veterinary medicine (DVM) degree.

Every physical therapy school and veterinary college has its own set of prerequisites. This is why it's important to figure out which route you want

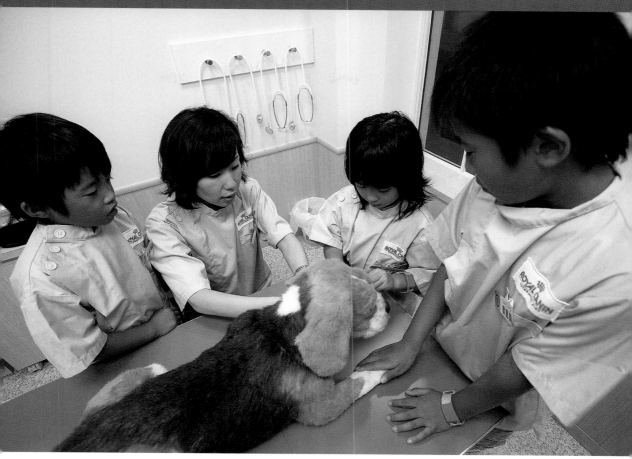

During a mock physical examination, this future veterinarian mimics drawing a blood sample from a dog doll. This work experience activity took place at KidZania in Tokyo, Japan.

to travel before going to college. You'll need to pick a track and the schools you plan to apply to, so you can fulfill the proper prerequisites. More than 200 colleges and universities in the nation offer physical therapy education programs accredited by the Commission on Accreditation in Physical Therapy Education. A complete list is available at the American Physical Therapy Association (APTA) website. You'll find career and admissions information there, too. The United States has twenty-eight accredited veterinary schools. Visit the Association of American Veterinary Colleges (AAVMC) website to view the list (most also have links to descriptor pages with complete details about prerequisites). Many of the prerequisites for veterinary college and physical therapy school overlap. Both curriculums require students to take biology, chemistry, physics, anatomy and physiology, statistics, English, and humanities. However, there are some differences. Pre-physical therapy students will take psychology and kinesiology, while pre-vet students are required to take genetics and more advanced chemistry courses.

Students earning a bachelor's degree are not required or advised to take any particular major, meaning a specific area of concentration, for either veterinary medicine or physical therapy. The key is to choose a major in an area that truly interests you. It's not uncommon for those seeking a career in animal physical rehabilitation to major in animal sciences, biology, kinesiology, chemistry, psychology, or zoology.

It's also important to earn good grades, especially if you are planning on going to veterinary school. Most veterinary colleges require applicants to have a 3.0 GPA, or B-average. The competition is steep, though. In 2011, the average GPA of incoming students was 3.5 or above at 20 out of the 28 accredited veterinary colleges in the United States.

The Physical Therapy Path

You've decided to study physical therapy! Once you've earned a bachelor's degree, it's time to apply to a university's physical therapy school. Advisors recommend applying to several schools. Look for a university that not only has an excellent physical therapy program, but also has a strong animal sciences department or veterinary college. The next step is to take the Graduate Record Examination (GRE), a required standardized written test, about six weeks before the application is due. Many physical therapy schools in the United States request students apply online through the Physical Therapist Centralized Application Service (PTCAS), while others have students apply directly to their programs. As part of their application,

Able Assistants

Don't have the finances for seven to eight years of college? You can still have a career in animal rehabilitation as a physical therapy assistant or veterinary technician. A physical therapy assistant works with patients under the supervision of a physical therapist. Likewise, a vet tech assists a rehabilitation veterinarian in treating patients (responsibilities also involve nursing duties, such as drawing blood, taking X-rays, performing lab tests, and assisting with surgeries). Be aware that vet techs and physical therapy assistants are not allowed to diagnose, evaluate, or develop treatment plans. Both jobs require completion of a two-year associate's degree program in their field of study at a community college. According to the U.S. Bureau of Labor Statistics, a physical therapy assistant earns about $50,000 a year, while a vet tech makes about $30,000.

students submit college transcripts (grades), GRE scores, work experience, and several letters of recommendation from college professors, teachers, and professionals they have worked with while gaining experience. Students will also be expected to answer questions or write a personal essay on their career goals. A university's physical therapy school typically has a committee that reviews all applications that are submitted directly to the program or through PTCAS. Many schools also require applicants to appear in person for an interview. A panel will ask questions pertaining to the applicant's knowledge of the subject area and passion for the career. The committee then selects students for admission.

Upon acceptance, students will spend three years earning their doctor of physical therapy (DPT) degree. The curriculum covers human anatomy, exercise physiology, orthopedics, neurology, motor skills, kinesiology, and more. Students learn how to examine, assess, and develop a treatment plan for

Saving for College

Figures from the American Physical Therapy Association reveal the total cost of attending physical therapy school can run anywhere between $20,000 and $156,000, depending on the school and whether or not a student applies to an in-state or out-of-state school. The full cost of attending four years of veterinary college falls between $155,000 and $240,000, according to the Association of American Veterinary Medical Colleges (this includes books, fees, health insurance, housing, and other living expenses). Keep in mind these figures are in addition to the cost of earning your bachelor's degree.

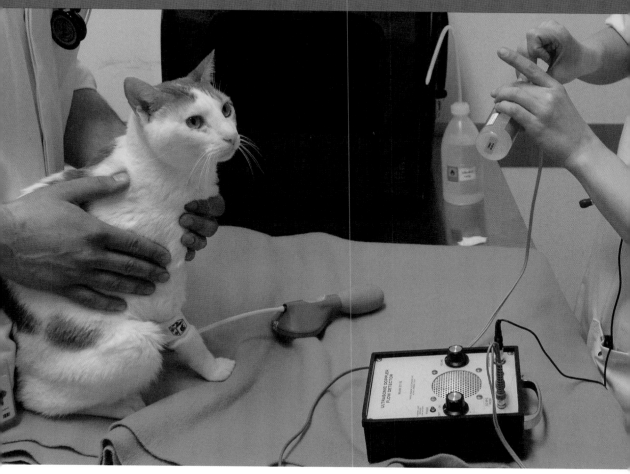

Veterinary students at the Dueppel animal clinic in Berlin, Germany, perform a blood test on a diabetic cat.

patients. They're taught various physical therapy techniques, such as therapeutic exercises, massage, and hydrotherapy. They learn to use equipment, like **lasers**, **ultrasound**, electrical stimulation, and thermotherapy. Students begin getting their first real-world experience through internships in their third semester. By their third year, three to five days per week are spent in a clinical setting working with patients under the supervision of professionals. All of the patients they work with are human, so students must look for outside opportunities to gain experience with animals. Professionals advise students to volunteer or do an internship at their school's animal sciences department or veterinary hospital. They should also do an externship or volunteer to work with an animal physical therapist, veterinarian, or wildlife rehabilitator.

The Veterinary Road

Is veterinary medicine the right track for you? If so, once your prerequisites are met, or you graduate from college, you will take the GRE exam and apply to veterinary colleges. Applications are submitted online through the AAVMC. On the application, students outline their work experience and write an essay about why they want to pursue a veterinary career. They also submit college transcripts, GRE scores, and two to four letters of recommendation (depending on the school) from college professors or other professionals that have supervised them. The AAVMC forwards every completed application to the appropriate

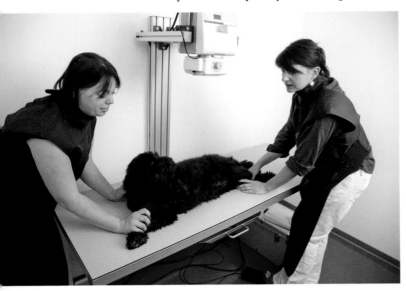

Veterinary technicians prepare a dog for X-rays.

college. An application committee at each school reviews the materials and selects students for admission. Some schools also require students to come to campus for a personal interview.

The competition to get into veterinary college in the United States is stiff.

In pursuit of the lifelong dream of becoming a veterinarian, Jennifer Simpson, left, and Heather Sheppard, right, examine a canine's cranial nervous system at University of Georgia College of Veterinary Medicine.

The AAVMC reports only about 45 percent of those who apply are accepted. A student that is accepted into veterinary school spends four years studying to become a doctor of veterinary medicine (DVM). The curriculum covers animal anatomy and diseases, surgery, imaging, including X-rays and **computerized tomography (CT) scans**, dental health, eye care, pain management, emergency care, aging, nutrition, and rehabilitation. Students learn to diagnose and treat illness and injury in small animals (cats and dogs), exotic animals (birds, reptiles, rodents, rabbits), **equines** (horses), and large animals (cattle and sheep). Most veterinary colleges also run teaching hospitals and clinics. These facilities give students experience treating animals under the guidance of a professional staff and faculty. Students usually begin working at a hospital or clinic in their third year of college.

In the last ten years, some veterinary schools in the United States have also opened rehabilitation centers for small animals and/or equines. Among

Future animal physical therapists and veterinarians engage in their studies at the University of Wisconsin School of Veterinary Medicine in Madison.

them are the University of Tennessee, Oregon State University, Louisiana State University, and the University of California, Davis. During their fourth year of veterinary school, students have the opportunity to spend a week or two working in the unit. It's a chance to become familiar with various physical therapy methods, such as hydrotherapy, massage, ultrasound, laser, electrical stimulation, and more. Those interested in a career in animal physical rehabilitation should spend as much time as possible in the rehabilitation center, or arrange to do an internship. All veterinary students may also choose, or be required, to do an externship. Typically lasting from three to eight weeks, an externship gives a student the chance to work in real-world conditions. Students should plan to do an externship at a veterinary clinic, equine rehabilitation center, wildlife sanctuary, or animal rescue organization.

A veterinary student at Penn State gives a puppy a shot.

Following graduation, a DVM may continue his/her education by becoming board certified in a specialty recognized by the AVMA (a veterinarian may do a specialty any time during his/her career). In 2011, the AVMA established a new specialty in sports medicine and rehabilitation, which is ideal for those pursuing a career in animal physical therapy. Board certification requires hands-on learning in a **residency** program under the direction of a veterinarian certified in the area of study. A residency lasts from three to four years. Before a veterinarian can become board certified, he/she must also pass a written exam.

The Training Continues

As you've learned, before medical graduates can legally practice, they must have a license. Physical therapists must take and pass the National Physical Therapy Exam, a computer-based test designed to ensure a professional is proficient in the subject area. Likewise, veterinarians must pass the North American Veterinary Licensing Exam, a 360-question multiple-choice test. Those in both professions may also be required to take a test on state laws and regulations.

Students at UC Davis School of Veterinary Medicine identify parasites by using microscopes during a lab session.

Many states also require that practitioners take **continuing education** classes every few years in order to renew their licenses. This additional coursework ensures professionals stay up to date on the latest research, technology, and advancements in their field. Coursework is accredited by professional organizations, such as the American Association of Veterinary State Boards or the American Veterinary Medical Association. Well-known and respected continuing education programs in animal physical therapy include the University of Tennessee's Certificate of Canine Rehabilitation Practitioner (CCRP) and the Certificate of Equine Physical Rehabilitation (CEPR), as well as the Certificate of Canine Rehabilitation Therapist (CCRT) offered by the Canine Rehabilitation Institute in Florida.

Professionals, particularly veterinarians, may also choose to pursue independent certification in specific treatment areas, such as massage, acupuncture, chiropractic, and herbal medicine from various schools. Animal physical rehabilitation practitioners understand the value of continuing to train throughout their career. They know that a skill they learn today could change a patient's life tomorrow.

THREE

Healers at Work

There are more than 275,000 veterinarians and physical therapists in the United States, but experts estimate that less than 1 percent of them work in animal physical rehabilitation. Of those who do, most are in private practice. They may be independent consultants, run their own clinics, or work at large hospitals or universities with other professionals.

Salaries in the field vary depending upon years of experience, employment location, and the size of the facility. Generally, those with a degree in physical therapy who work with animals can expect to earn between $60,000 and $80,000 per year (about the same as if they were treating humans). Veterinarians make, on average, about $82,000 per year, according the U.S. Department of Labor.

A physical therapist who works with animals doesn't do things much differently from one who works with humans. "Today, just about everything we can do for people with physical therapy we can do for dogs and cats," says Dr. David Levine. "Now we start therapy for an animal the day after surgery, just as you would for a person, and we're able to get full range of motion and functionality back."

(Opposite) This Bengal kitten is being treated at a pet hospital in La Condesa, Mexico City, Mexico.

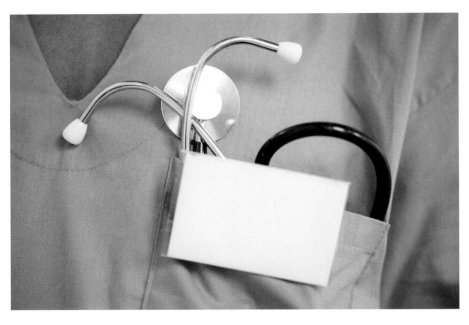

The Name Game

In all fifty U.S. states, the two-word term "physical therapist" is protected by law. It can only be used by someone who holds a physical therapy license. Therefore, veterinarians who do animal physical therapy must officially refer to themselves in another way, such as animal physical rehabilitation practitioners or animal physical rehabilitation veterinarians.

A pair of physically healthy and active dogs play ball on the beach.

On the Job

As in human medicine, where primary care doctors refer patients to physical therapists, so too do veterinarians put their patients in the care of animal physical rehabilitators. Referral to a practitioner usually follows an injury, surgery, or the diagnosis of an illness. Health issues that can benefit from physical therapy include arthritis, joint replacements, fractures, muscle or tendon injuries, neuromuscular diseases, amputation, hip dysplasia, back problems, and nerve damage. Out of shape, obese, and aging pets may also be good candidates for physical therapy. Referral by a veterinarian is an important step in the

Dogs love to jump, run, and play, which means accidents, including a broken leg, are bound to happen.

process. It ensures that the patient has been thoroughly examined and there are no other health problems or complications that might hinder recovery. In turn, the physical therapist will keep in close contact with the veterinarian to update him/her on the patient's progress.

At the first meeting with a new patient and owner, a physical therapist does an evaluation. He/she reviews medical records including X-rays, lab tests, and other information sent by the referring veterinarian. The therapist asks the owner about the animal's home environment, exercise habits, behaviors, and diet. He/she performs an exam to discover how much strength and mobility the patient has and identifies any pain issues. An animal isn't able to tell the therapist where it hurts, but that doesn't mean he/she can't communicate. An animal that's hurting may pant, lick itself repeatedly, have dilated pupils, whimper, or turn to look at the therapist. "My greatest tool as a PT is my eyes," explains Amie Hesbach, a physical therapist at the Massachusetts Veterinary Referral Hospital, north of Boston. "I have to be observant and always be paying attention to what the animal is trying to communicate."

Once the evaluation is complete, the therapist tailors a treatment program for recovery. This plan spells out goals the physical therapist would like to help the patient achieve over a set length of time. Treatment goals may include increasing range of motion, developing motor skills, strengthening or stretching muscles, decreasing pain and inflammation, and improving fitness. Preventing future injury is also important. Sometimes, the plan may include fitting the patient with **orthotics**, such as braces, slings, and splints. Equipment can help to support an injured limb while it heals, encourage proper use of the limb, or correct a deformity. **Prostheses**, or artificial limbs, and carts or wheelchairs for paralyzed patients are an option, too. The physical therapist will make sure all equipment is fitted correctly and functioning properly. With a treatment program in place, it's time to get to work!

After the repair of two broken legs, this St. Bernard recuperates in the sunshine.

The Journey Back

Frequently, an animal is an outpatient, meaning its owner will bring it into the clinic to work with a physical therapist as directed. It's not unusual for a practitioner to see five or more patients each day. A therapy session may last for less than ten minutes up to an hour, depending upon where the patient is in the treatment process. A physical therapist may work alone or with help from other practitioners. To help patients reach their treatment goals, physical therapists have an arsenal of tools and techniques at their disposal. Some of the common methods they

Born to Run

When racing, sporting, or working horses get injured, their owners turn to equine physical therapists for help. These practitioners use many of the same techniques as those who work with small animals, as well as a few others, such as cold water spas, solarium (infrared lights), and **hyperbaric oxygen therapy.** In hyperbaric therapy, the horse is placed in an enclosed, pressurized chamber where it breathes air filled with higher than normal concentrations of oxygen. The additional oxygen helps to speed the body's own healing process. Someone interested in this career should follow the same educational route as a small animal physical therapy practitioner and do an externship with an equine rehabilitation facility. Those entering the profession with physical therapy and veterinary degrees can expect an average starting salary of $40,000 to $60,000 per year. However, it is a highly competitive area within the field.

Jewel readies for her active therapeutic exercise with lead K9 rehabilitator Cori Baldwin at the St. Francis Rehabilitation Center in Williamsburg, Virginia.

use are massage, therapeutic exercise, and hydrotherapy.

The term "massage" comes from the Arabic word *mass*, meaning "to press." A physical therapist will use his/her hands to rub, knead, or stroke the body's soft tissues. Massage helps loosen and stretch muscles, improves range of motion, and stimulates blood circulation to aid in healing. It also eases pain, swelling, and stiffness. Plus, because most animals enjoy the process, it can reduce anxiety and tension. Massage often works well with cats, which are, by nature, less active than dogs and can sometimes be less cooperative.

Therapeutic exercises are various exercises designed to improve range of motion, muscle strength, balance, gait, and fitness. Therapeutic exercises may be passive or active. A passive exercise is one where the therapist moves the limb. An active exercise is one where the animal does most or all of the work, such as walking, climbing stairs, or exercises like puppy squats (the dog goes from standing to sitting and then back up to a standing position again). Therapeutic exercise may also involve gym equipment, such as land treadmills, physio balls, balance boards, tension bands, small trampolines, or low

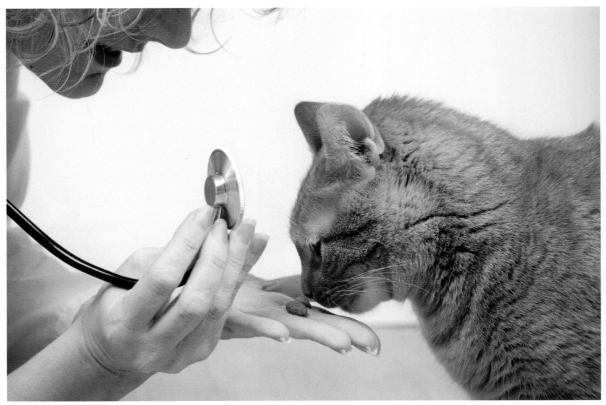

Some pets are shy about visits to the vet's office but open up when offered a treat.

rails. The therapist safely guides the patient through each exercise, providing support for the body and assistance as necessary.

Hydrotherapy exercise is done in the water. Because water bears up to 60 percent of an animal's weight, many exercises that are hard to do on land are much easier in the water. The therapist may place a dog or cat on a water treadmill, a piece of equipment where the lower half of the body is submerged (the higher the water level, the more weight is supported). Sometimes the therapist will sit behind the animal to provide support and help with movement. Swimming pools, resistance pools, or whirlpools may also be utilized. During hydrotherapy, animals usually wear life vests. They are under constant supervision for safety reasons.

More treatment options for animal physical rehabilitation practitioners include thermotherapy, electrical stimulation, ultrasound, laser, acupuncture, and chiropractic.

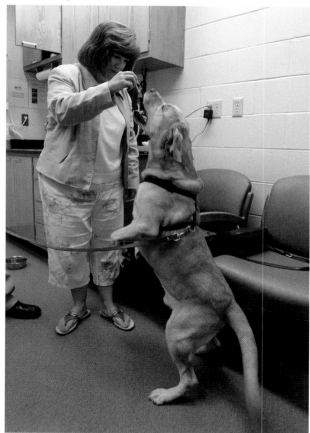

Grommit, an 8-year-old yellow Labrador, gets a treat after his examination.

In working with patients, safety and comfort are key concerns. A physical therapist takes things slowly, never forcing an animal into a position that may cause discomfort. The patient should not experience pain. To build trust and foster cooperation, a therapist must be kind, encouraging, and even a bit clever. "It can take some creativity to get an animal to do what you want," explains Dr. Christie Carlo, a rehabilitation veterinarian. She says to get a dog to work on the treadmill she might have to entice him with a toy or a cup of frozen peanut butter. Cats can be more of a challenge. Some respond to a toy, catnip, or tuna, but others, she may have to trick into therapy. "Most cats like being petted slowly from front to back and will arch their backs when they are rubbed," explains Dr. Carlo. "As they stretch they have to balance and tighten their core. You are always thinking about your patient; how to incorporate what he needs to be doing with what he likes to do."

A therapist may also give pet owners exercises to do with their animals between visits. "Pet owners are very fearful of the unknown," says Amie Hesbach. "Their dog can't tell them how they are feeling. If I can give an owner some things to do with their pet that are positive, productive, and non-threatening, it eases their mind. And it helps increase the bond between animal and human."

After each visit, the physical therapist records the animal's progress. He/she also updates the referring veterinarian as necessary. Some patients may require only a few therapy sessions, while others may need several months to recover. The good news is that physical therapy for animals is quite effective. A small percentage may end up with some limitations, but nearly all patients return to leading healthy, active lives.

A pair of Jack Russell terriers shows off in the sand.
This breed is known to thrive on action and adventure.

FOUR

Meet the Animal Physical Therapists

A three-year-old Thoroughbred horse named The Factor had quickly risen to the top of the horse-racing world. Winning race after race, the colt looked as if he might be a contender for the Kentucky Derby. That's when things began to unravel. After recovering from throat surgery and a hairline fracture in his ankle, the horse made a poor showing in a couple of races. His veterinarian and trainer couldn't find a reason as to why one of the fastest horses in the world was losing. So they sent The Factor to Kirsten Johnson, a top equine rehabilitation therapist and owner of the Kentucky Equine Sports Medicine and Rehabilitation Center. "Horses love to run. They don't just wake up and decide not to compete," explains Kirsten. "Pain or something else is going on. It's my job to put the pieces of the puzzle together. In this case, I could see when the horse came through the doors he wasn't happy. He needed a break."

(Above) Many Thoroughbred stallions suffer common injuries and ailments including bleeding, splints, and bone chips in the knee and ankle.
(Opposite) While most large animal vets treat a variety of livestock species, some choose to focus on offering services exclusively for equine patients.

Many animal physical therapists use holistic medicines and techniques in animal treatments because they are gentle and incorporate patient well-being and stress reduction.

Kirsten developed a treatment program for the top athlete, consisting of hyperbaric oxygen treatments, controlled exercise, a nutritional plan, and plenty of rest. A month later, the horse "was a different being." Kirsten could tell her patient was eager to train and run again. And she was right. His first race back, The Factor nearly broke a track record.

More than a thousand horses a year, from as far away as New Zealand and South Africa, are sent by their veterinarians to Kirsten's facility just outside of Lexington, Kentucky. Some horses come to recover from a serious injury, while others, like The Factor, need time away from athletic

Know Your Stuff

Kirsten says a love of horses is a start, but isn't enough for a career as an equine rehabilitation therapist. The work can be physically demanding and the days long. You need to be able to communicate well with veterinarians, trainers, and owners. You must also learn how to handle the financial side of the business. She recommends students spend time shadowing an equine therapist to experience what it's truly like. Her facility offers two internship programs. One is for high school and early college students (minimum age to apply is 17). The other is a live-in dorm internship for college students studying veterinary medicine and physical therapy.

competition. Walk through the fifty-six-stall barn and you'll see various horses from backyard pets to grand prix show jumpers. But status doesn't matter to Kirsten and her staff of four (plus interns). "Whether he's worth $500 or $7 million, every horse gets the same respect here," she says. "Every horse gets our love and attention and the benefit of everything we know."

And what Kirsten knows is plenty. A horse lover since childhood, she started her career in equine rehabilitation more than twenty years ago. It was seeing the lack of proper therapy for injured horses that fueled her passion. "A human athlete goes to an orthopedic surgeon and he's going to say 'your recovery is only as good as the work you put into it afterward,'" she says. "It didn't make sense to me for a horse to stand in a stall and then to be turned out after a week or two to run and jump on an injury. I just thought there had to be a better way to do things." She began learning as much as she could about the field and working with veterinarians. In 2001, she was ready to run a large facility of her own and bought the training center.

A horse's stay at the center lasts, on average, about 45 days (some may come for just a few days, and others may remain for a year). "Watching these horses go back and compete, to go on to do what it is they are meant to do and do it well, is a great satisfaction for me," says Kirsten. "I still walk through the doors every day and think 'I am living my dream.'" What's her favorite part of the job? "I'd say getting a kiss on the nose from a horse that is going to race in the Breeder's Cup is pretty amazing!"

Walk on the Wild Side

In her twenty-four years as a physical therapist, the last half working with animals, Dr. Jackie Woelz has amassed an impressive list of patients. She's treated hawks that were hurt after flying into power lines and police dogs injured in pursuit of suspects. She's helped ferrets, rabbits, horses, sheep, and even elephants!

Helping Gentle Giants

California's Performing Animal Welfare Society (PAWS) is an organization that rescues mistreated and retired captive wildlife from circuses and zoos. When elephants at the sanctuary were ailing, PAWS turned to Dr. Woelz for help. Elephants often develop severe arthritis prematurely from standing on cement while in confinement. To help relieve joint pain and decrease inflammation, Dr. Woelz used a laser on her pachyderm patients. "The elephants seemed to appreciate the effects," she recalls. "The second time I went out to visit them, one that I had treated previously came right over and extended her leg so that I could easily reach it with the laser. They are amazing, highly intelligent, calculating creatures."

Many veterinarians and animal physical therapists grew up raising and caring for animals such as this ashy storm-petrel chick.

Jackie grew up raising all kinds of critters at home. After earning a bachelor's degree in biology, she worked at the San Diego Zoo, Scripps Institution of Oceanography, and the Monterey Bay Aquarium. In 1991, she got her physical therapy degree and began treating people in clinics and hospitals. But her passion for animals led her to wonder why the same physical therapy methods that worked so well on humans weren't being made available to animals. "I realized that there was a tremendous void in veterinary medicine and no one was guiding patients through the recovery phase after injury, surgery, or disability," she says. "It made sense to me to pursue this with the local veterinarians. Once they understood what I was proposing, we started working together."

Dr. Woelz was the founding therapist for the Physical Rehabilitation Service at UC Davis School of Veterinary Medicine. Opened in 2004, it was among the first animal rehabilitation units at a university veterinary teaching hospital in the country. Fourth-year veterinary students may choose to spend time in the unit learning physical therapy techniques to treat small animals.

Dr. Woelz is now in private practice and receives referrals from veterinarians, zoos, wildlife sanctuaries, shelters, and veterinary schools. She says she enjoys the collaboration between professionals almost as much as she loves her hard-working patients. "Animals are very positive and they want to get better," she says. "They never complain and they seem to appreciate and use what they have, not what they don't have. And a tail wag is the best 'thank you!'"

FIVE

A Promising Future

A determined problem-solver, Dr. Christie Carlo admits she "doesn't like to lose." Yet four years ago, that's what she felt was happening far too frequently in her veterinary practice. "Someone would come in with a lame pet and I would give [the animal] pain medication and send them on their way," she explains. "But they'd often come back and say 'this isn't helping,' and I didn't know what I could do." Dr. Carlo then decided to study animal rehabilitation, and it changed the way she practiced medicine. "I went from having few options to having a whole range of them—massage, laser therapy, acupuncture, chiropractic," she says. "Now I have many more ways to help pets get better."

One of just two certified canine rehabilitation veterinarians in the state of Iowa, Dr. Carlo's story is a good example of why the field of animal physical rehabilitation has such a bright future. As more veterinarians incorporate physical therapy into their practices, it gains wider acceptance and understanding from the entire profession. Veterinarians, in turn, are educating millions of pet owners on its value.

The U.S. Department of Labor reports that overall, the future job market for veterinarians and physical therapists is strong. Both fields are expected

(Opposite) A veterinarian is an important ally in maintaining a pet's health.

Post-operative care techniques are important in terms of the pet's comfort, safety, and recuperation.

to grow faster than the average of all other professions. Projections indicate the nation will require 39 percent more physical therapists and 36 percent more veterinarians by 2020. In animal physical rehabilitation, however, there are some issues that cast shadows on this positive outlook. More physical therapists will be required to treat the aging baby boom population, which means most of the physical therapy openings will be for those that involve working with humans, not animals. For veterinarians, predications show more than 20,000 new animal doctors will be needed before the decade's end. But with 2,700 veterinary graduates entering the job market every year, in ten years there will be more veterinarians than jobs. On the up side, 70% of new veterinarians are choosing to pursue small animal medicine. With 20,000 such practices already in existence, those who choose animal rehabilitation may have a competitive edge. "Animal rehabilitation is an expanding field," says Dr. Carlo. "With the job market saturated in small animal practice, the more people who realize that there are opportunities in special interest and [choose to] diversify, the better off we'll be."

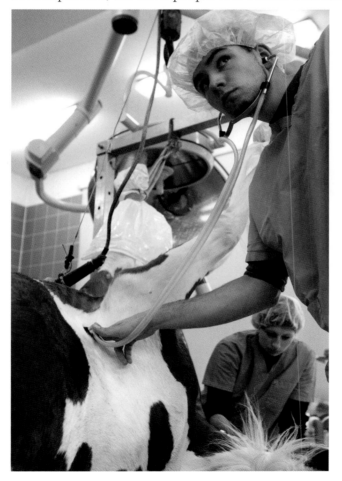

A horse undergoes arthroscopic surgery at the Research Center for Medical Technology and Biotechnology in Bad Langensalza, Germany.

Breaking New Ground

Most experts agree that for animal physical therapy to truly flourish as a career field, the two major challenges we discussed in Chapter Two, licensing laws and education, must be fully addressed. Unlike the United States, the United Kingdom recognizes animal physical therapy as a legal profession. Experts say it's time

Don't Take Shortcuts

As animal physical therapy grows in popularity, more independent schools are popping up to offer "certified" training in the field. The trend has professionals worried. These trade-school-like programs are attractive because many allow students to graduate in one year or less. But experts say one year, or even two, is not nearly enough time to garner the kind of skills and experience required to be a competent animal physical therapist. Also, the term "certified" is vague. It can simply mean that you have completed a particular program, not that the course is accredited by a professional organization, such as the Commission on Accreditation in Physical Therapy Education or the AVMA. Experts say someone who chooses a quick route over an accredited college or university program could end up putting their animal patients in jeopardy.

A future veterinarian examines a dog doll during her work experience activity at KidZania in Tokyo, Japan.

for the United States to step up and do the same. Terms must be clarified and state laws changed to allow qualified animal physical rehabilitation practitioners to freely practice in every state without fear of losing their license. Also, in the United Kingdom, students are able to directly train to become animal physiotherapists (their term for physical therapists). They do not first have to become veterinarians or physical therapists for humans. New Zealand, Australia, and South Africa also offer similar educational programs. Academic advisors say it's only a matter of time before colleges and universities in the United States follow suit and create

53

A cocker spaniel puppy shows affection.

programs that offer students a track to receive a degree and license in the field. But no one can be sure when this will occur.

What we do know is that as the profession grows, so will opportunities to be part of the educational process. Skilled and experienced practitioners will be needed to teach at universities, veterinary colleges (and their hospitals and rehabilitation centers), and continuing education programs. In 2002, Dr. Janet Van Dyke founded the Canine Rehabilitation Institute (CRI) in Florida after "realizing that my field was sorely lacking in training." Accredited by the American Association of Veterinary State Boards, the school teaches canine physical therapy to veterinarians, veterinary technicians, physical therapists, and physical therapist assistants. Dr. Van Dyke taps only the best and the brightest for her faculty. "Everyone who teaches for CRI is an independent contractor who runs their own rehabilitation practice and flies in to teach their particular

Getting Back in the Game

A decade ago, a dog that lost the use of a limb would likely face amputation. Since then, veterinary science has learned that what works for people can work for animals, too. Animal physical therapists can now fit their amputee patients with prostheses made of lightweight, yet sturdy materials, like plastic or carbon composite. Some limbs are even waterproof! Although dogs tend to be the most common patients, cats, horses, and even farm animals can benefit, too. With a little physical therapy, most animals adapt quite well to their new equipment.

area of expertise for us," she explains. CRI also has locations in Maryland and Colorado (in cooperation with the College of Veterinary Medicine & Biomedical Sciences at Colorado State University), and is expanding to offer courses in the United Kingdom and Australia.

Puppy Love

Americans are passionate about their pets and, if the amount of money we spend on them is any indicator of our emotions, our affection is growing. According to the American Pet Products Association National Pet Owner survey, in 2012, pet owners spent $53 billion to give their animals the best in food, toys, grooming, boarding, and veterinary care. That's $2 billion more than they spent the previous year. Trends also show that more pet owners are making sure their pets have preventative care, such as regular vaccinations, checkups, and dental cleanings. Many owners are also opting for advanced services for their pets. Demand is growing for joint replacements, orthotics, prostheses, and physical therapy.

Professionals say in the years to come animal physical rehabilitation is likely to become a standard part of veterinary care, especially as more pet owners learn of its benefits. Dog owner Lisa Owens has seen firsthand the dramatic difference it can make. She remembers what life was like for Asta, her 11-year-old greyhound, just two years ago. Diagnosed with a spinal condition that caused severe back pain and lameness, the retired racing dog could barely walk. "She had to be carried up and down the stairs," recalls Lisa. "Sometimes she needed help lying down. Things were not good." Then Asta's veterinarian and neurologist suggested trying acupuncture to reduce pain and stimulate healing. After a month of acupuncture a couple of times per week from a certified veterinarian, Lisa noticed Asta was moving better. Soon, the dog was walking on her own and even enjoying an occasional

Although fast, agile, and athletic, the Italian Greyhound's slim build and short coat makes it somewhat fragile.

short run. "We honestly thought those activities were behind her, so her improved vitality makes us all very happy," says Lisa, who still takes Asta for acupuncture treatments twice per month. "These days she is strong enough to pull me where she wants with her leash!"

For those who choose a career in animal physical rehabilitation, there is satisfaction not only in helping patients but people, too. "The doggie kisses are a great perk of the job," says Julie Stuart, the physical therapist you met at the beginning of the book. "But seeing the look of relief on a pet owner's face when I say 'don't worry, we will get this dog walking again,' is absolutely incredible. It's a big part of why I do what I do. And why I love it so much."

Glossary

acupuncture   the ancient Chinese medical practice of inserting small needles just under the skin at various points of the body to treat illness, pain, and swelling

canine   relating to dogs

chiropractic   a therapeutic system based upon the interactions of the spine and nervous system in which treatment involves adjusting the segments of the spinal column

computerized tomography (CT) scans   a series of X-rays taken from different angles that are combined and processed by the computer to give more detail than a standard X-ray

continuing education   classes professionals take following their initial training to advance their knowledge and skills

diagnose   to determine the cause or nature of an illness or injury through examination

equine   relating to horses

externship   an off-campus, supervised, work-experience program for college students

hydrotherapy   physical therapy done in the water

hyperbaric oxygen therapy   therapy that uses a pressurized chamber to deliver high levels of oxygen to the bloodstream to promote healing

internship   paid or unpaid student programs in a professional workplace, in which students receive college credit in return for their work

kinesiology	the science or study of how the human body moves
lasers	devices that emit a type of light; low-level lasers are used by physical therapists to relieve a patient's pain and/or stimulate healing
orthotics	splints, slings, braces, and other equipment used to help stabilize the body and allow for normal function
polio	short for poliomyelitis, a viral disease that inflames the brain stem and spinal cord and can lead to paralysis
practicum	the section of a class that consists of practical, hands-on work
prerequisites	courses students are required to take for admittance to a program
prostheses	artificial limbs
residency	a program in which a doctor or veterinarian joins a medical practice or works at a university in a salaried position for a set period to gain advanced training in a specialty
therapeutic exercise	exercises designed to help restore function and mobility to the body's joints and muscles
thermotherapy	using heat or cold to aid in healing
ultrasound	the use of sound waves to create internal images of the body

Find Out More

Books

Field, Shelly. *Career Opportunities: Working with Animals.* New York: Checkmark Books, 2012.

Hollow, Michael C. and William O. Rives. *The Everything Guide to Working with Animals.* Avon, MA: Adams Media, 2010.

Ryan-Flynn, Mary Susan. *What Can I Do Now? Animal Careers.* New York: Ferguson, 2010.

Trueit, Trudi Strain. *Veterinarian.* New York: Cavendish Square, 2014.

Websites

Association of American Veterinary Medical Colleges

www.aavmc.org

Log on to see a complete list of national and international accredited veterinary colleges, along with descriptor pages that explain prerequisites and application requirements. You can also explore careers in veterinary medicine, find pre-vet resources, and learn more about the veterinary school application process.

American Association of Rehabilitation Veterinarians (AARV)

www.rehabvets.org

Founded in 2007, the AARV seeks to connect professionals and advance the field of rehabilitation medicine. Learn more about what rehabilitation veterinarians do, the conditions they treat, and the various methods they use in their work.

American Physical Therapy Association

www.apta.org

Explore career options, watch a video, and discover more about the educational track for physical therapists and physical therapist assistants. You can also find accredited schools in the United States and learn the exact process for admissions.

Index

Page numbers in **boldface** are illustrations.

About the Author

Trudi Strain Trueit is the author of more than eighty fiction and nonfiction books for young readers. A former television journalist and weather forecaster, she enjoys writing about career exploration, health, weather, earth science, and history. Look for her other titles in the Careers with Animals series: *Veterinarian, Animal Trainer,* and *Wildlife Conservationist.* Trueit has a bachelor's degree in broadcast journalism and lives in Everett, Washington, with her husband and their two cats. Read more about Trueit and her books at www.truditrueit.com.